The Marks of a Christian

Earl Robinson

Clay City, Indiana

ISBN 0-88019-179-1

Printed by
Old Paths Tract Society Inc.
Shoals, Indiana 47581

Preface

As far as Christ is concerned, there are two dangers which everyone must face. The first is that those who are not Christians will never turn to Him for forgiveness. The second is that those who are Christians may, at some time in their life, depart from Him. And this departure could be the result of fears and doubts as to whether one was really a Christian in the first place. Or the Christian had no doubts of his conversion at a definite time in the past. Yet his reaction, due to some fierce temptation or crisis of life, he comes to doubt his present standing with Christ. It should not, however, be forgotten that doubts and fears as to one's relationship with Jesus can creep over the brightest faith.

To counter-act such false doubts, fears, and disbeliefs, and also to help one determine his true position with Christ, *The Marks of a Christian* was written. Evidence for this purpose has been obtained from true Christians' experiences and the Scriptures. This evidence will give those who may be struggling in the wreck of their religious life, a standard by which they can measure their standing with Christ or by which they can judge as to whether they are really a child of God.

Also, deceptions can be a real problem with respect to one's relationship with Christ. Different ways have been given by which a person can be deceived in believing he is a Christian when in fact he is not. Also, one who once displayed a bright Christian experience, yet strayed away, can be deceived in believing that he still retains a saving faith in Christ.

It is, therefore, our hope and prayer that this booklet will help steady those of wavering faith, and also reveal to others their true position in regard to their relationship with Jesus.

Earl Robinson
Clay City, Indiana

Contents

Who Is a Christian? 7

The Evidence of the New Birth 10

The Marks of a Christian from Scripture 15

Deception Pertaining to the New Birth 31

CHAPTER ONE

Who Is a Christian?

"Beneath all the definitions (of the work of the Holy Spirit in regeneration) there remains the mystery of life, and the action of the Spirit upon spirit. What this spiritually vivifying (to give life to) touch of God is no man will ever know. The region lies deep within us, the Agent, the Holy Spirit, acts unseen,—and apparently not desiring to be seen in his inner workings. Thus we have no material for a definition from within. But this obscurity need not trouble us, for it is the only obscurity that hangs over all inner spiritual processes." *An Outline of Christian Theology*, p. 397.

"He that has the son of God has life; and he that has not the Son of God has not life." I John 5:12.

The word "Christian" has been in the vocabulary of languages for some 2,000 years. It was first used as a term of derision or ridicule to identify a small group of people in that day. It was first used in the city of Antioch. As time moved on, the name "Christian" became more respectable. This was due to their courage, meekness, and sincerity of their behavior. It is clear, then, that these people possessed those distinguishing characteristics which set them apart from the non-Christian world.

A Christian can be defined in various ways. For example, one whose attitudes and conduct are formed and motivated by Jesus Christ is a Christian. This definition is correct as far as it goes. However, before a more comprehensive definition can be given, the word "life" must first be considered.

Life is one of those words for which no precise definition can be given. Like electricity and gravitation, we don't really know what it is. However, there are two definitions which will help us to understand this mysterious force called life. First, "life is the sum total of those forces that resist death." The plant, for example, utilizing sunshine, air, food, and water will grow and produce fruit when life is present. When the relationship between these elements and their environment cease to exist, death and decay is the result. To behold any living thing is to see the creeping hand of death. Death, then, not life, holds sway over every thing on earth. "Life is, therefore, a temporal endowment which holds in check, for a time, death's destructive forces.

Second, again, life has been defined as a close relationship, or correspondence between living things and their surroundings or environment. When the air without, for example, and the lungs within, work in harmony the result is life, if all the other organs of the body are in working order. If this relationship should cease, due to some defect in the lungs, death is the result. Or this correspondence can be broken if air is prevented from reaching the lungs, even though the lungs are in perfect condition. To live, then, to maintain the lowest or highest of conscious existence for any living form, it is necessary for that form, be it a bacteria or a man, to maintain an unbroken contact with its environment. No living thing, therefore, can live apart from its environment. To state the idea in different words, for a plant, a man, or an animal to exercise the functions of living, there must be a constant harmonious relationship between them and their environment. A fish cannot live out of the water; a man cannot breathe oxygen in the water. This discussion of physical life now leads to a question of great practical importance. That form of life on earth possessed by man is superior to all others. The question is, does there exist in the universe or outer space a life superior to that of man? Indeed, such a life exists. It has been known for some 2,000 years. This Life, vastly superior to all known kinds, moves, like the wind, over earth's population and finds a dwelling place in the hearts of men. This life has been identified. It is known as the Christ-life or the life possessed by Jesus. To learn more about this type of life, that changes the attitudes, conduct and character of men, consider the following four verses from the New Testament.

(1) John 5:26, "For just as the Father has life in himself, so has he granted the Son to have life in himself." Jesus' physical life came to an end at His death. However,

He was in possession of another type of life which did not depend for its continuous existence upon a physical environment. Remember that our bodies are alive because every moment we are in vital contact with and sustained by a physical environment. The life possessed by Jesus depends on nothing outside of Himself. (John 5:26).

(2) John 5:12, "Whosoever has the Son has life; and whosoever does not have the Son does not have life." The great truth here to bear in mind is the Christ-life can be imparted to people living on this planet. The gulf that has separated people from the spiritual world has been crossed by the death of Jesus. They way, then, is open by which the life of Christ can be bestowed, by the agency of the Spirit, upon any person who will submit to Christ.

(3) Galatians 2:20, "I have been crucified with Christ, and it is no longer I that live, but Christ lives in me." Notice the words, "Christ lives in me." Christ, as a person, ascended to heaven. He is there now. When Paul speaks of "Christ living in me" he, of course, is referring to the life of Christ which is synonymous with Christ. The new birth and physical birth, it should be known, differ in an important aspect. In physical birth, the baby is a separate distinct person from its parents. In spiritual birth this is not true. When the Life of Christ comes to abide with me, no new person is born in the sense of a separate distinct person. My nature is changed—desires, attitudes and so on, but not my personality.

The question, who is a Christian? can now be answered. Since Spiritual Life exists in the person of Christ, and since this life can and is imparted to men through the agency of the Holy Spirit, a Christian is one who possesses this life. Let there be no doubt, no idea of some kind hallucination here. For in spite of deceptions and hypocrisy on the part of some, there are those to whom has come this wonderful, mysterious form of life. This life in fact is a divine Person, or Christ. The result of this indwelling is a changed disposition or character from the one who hates, steals and murders to the good moral person. Whatever else, then, a person may be, if he does not possess the life of Christ, he cannot in the nature of the case, he cannot be a Christian.

CHAPTER TWO

The Evidence of the New Birth

"It was October 21, 1969, and I bear witness that on that day heaven came down and glory filled my soul—the Spirit of God purged me and I knew the Holy Spirit was present in me, cleansing me—. As I walked out of that chapel, I was still in man's prison, but the prison I had been born in was gone and I walked out into a free place where God's peace reigns—." *Holes in Time*, p. 188.

"For the kingdom of God is not meat and drink but doing right, peace and joy in the Holy Spirit." (Romans 14:17).

In a previous chapter, a Christian was defined as one to whom Christ by His Spirit has come to dwell. This experience is known by such names as conversion, the new birth, and born again. It should be remembered that the coming of Spiritual Life to the soul is not a growth or a process. In keeping with the advent of all life, Christ coming to the soul is but the work of a moment. One moment a person is "dead in trespasses and sin," the next there has been imparted to him the very Life of God. The purpose of this chapter is to give evidence of that first moment when the seeker is conscious of the Presence of God in his heart. This evidence is all important. "Nothing short of certainty can satisfy, or ought to, a soul whose eternal destiny is the question in debate."

One of the most important verses of Scripture bearing on this point is found in Romans 8:16. The Spirit assures our spirit that we are the children of God. And this witness has its beginning at the moment of the New Birth. This witness or assurance as defined by John Wesley, the founder of Methodism, is an inward impression on the soul of the believer whereby the Spirit of God testifies to our spirits or (understanding) that we are the children of God. These impressions are made on the sensibilities (feelings, emotions, desires) and the intellect (reason, memory, knowing). The agency which produces these impressions is the Holy Spirit. When the keys of a piano are touched by a master musician, the result or effect is a flow of melodies pleasing to those who hear them. And when the living Spirit touches the keys of the soul, the impressions experienced are evidence that the seeker has been born into the kingdom of God.

The question is, what are the impressions made by the Spirit upon the seeker's heart or inner life? To know the answer to this question is to possess a conscious knowledge of Christ's presence in the soul. To find an answer it is not only necessary to search Scripture, but also the field of human experience. There have been, then, those in all ages who affirm that an outside power lifted them to a higher plane of living by the touch of a divine hand. Below are testimonies of those who experienced a marvelous change in their attitudes and dispositions. An analysis of these experiences will reveal what elements in these impressions are evidence of the moment of the New Birth.

1. "But the next morning it (the Bible) was a new book. The light of heaven shone on every page. I was in a new world. It was the most delicious joy I have ever known." *They Call Him Mr. Moody*, p. 53.

2. "I fell down at his feet—and made such confessions as I could with my choked utterance—no words can describe the wonderful love that was shed abroad in my heart." *Memories of Charles G. Finney*, p. 16-17.

3. "I was finding out for the first time the sweetness and joy of God." *Conversion of Billy Graham*, p. 53.

The four testimonies given below are those of a medical doctor, a prostitute, a minister and a criminal lawyer. They are found in *Evidence that Demands a Verdict*, by Josh McDowell, except the criminal lawyer.

Medical Doctor
1. "My drinking had become uncontrollable—on May 21, 1959, I was on a business trip and under deep conviction as I drove along. I prayed for God to save me—but it was not until I said, 'Anything you want me to do Lord, I will do,' could I believe. Then the indescribable experience occured. Tears of joy ran down my cheeks as the tremendous load of sin was lifted. I have not been tempted since to

take another drop of alcohol.''—Vernon Phillips

Prostitute

2. Author Blissit is speaking. "It was one of the most unexpected turnabouts I have ever encountered. Linda got down on her knees and prayed; her tears washed the mascara in streaks down her face. After we prayed, she looked up and her eyes sparkled. 'I am saved,' she said, joyously. 'Jesus has found me and I am going back to my baby.' "

Minister

3. "We decided to study Jesus without any help of any kind—It began to dawn on me that if I would put myself in God's hands—that this would be equal to doing God's will—He was calling me to act. The light broke upon me. I wept like a child calling out to my wife: 'I have missed it. All these years I have preached only ethics, social and personal, but not the gospel. The gospel is the living Christ who has come to live in me. He has liberated me. He has assured me my sins are forgiven.' "

Criminal

4. "—Get in big shot, we'll be back for you in fifty years (a lawyer sentenced to 50 years in prison). They slammed the door as I walked into the little cell. Oh, my God, what if there really is a God? I got down on my knees and cried out: 'God, if you will give me one more start, and one more life, I will never ask for anything else.' I could just feel the warmth, love, kindness, gentleness and peace." *Miracles in Prison Cells*—Chaplain Ray.

Here are seven descriptions of the moment of the new birth. They were given by those who represent the highest moral standard—Graham, Finney, and Moody—and those who represent the lowest moral standard—the criminal, the lawyer, and the prostitute.

These seven are also representatives of those in all ages who can testify to the assurance of that moment when they became conscious of a change within. They knew that an outside spiritual force or power had made its entrance into their souls.

First, let us notice just what they felt or what impressions were produced by their experience. Four expressed emotions of joy; two, Rev. Finney and the lawyer, experienced a deep love for the Saviour; and all stated or implied that there came to them a wonderful, peaceful state of mind not experienced before. Other terms used to describe their experiences were: a burden lifted, a gentleness, a conscious knowledge of sin forgiven, and I wept like a child. It can therefore be said that the outflowing from the sensibilities of peace, comfort, love and joy are the evidence that one has received the Life of Christ which are found in every true conversion.

Second, as a result of their experiences their came a change in desires, sentiments, and attitudes. A desire is created when we want some object or person. Sentiments are deep personal attachments of people. They have in them emotional and intellectual elements. For example, a man desires a wife. Connected with this is the desire for a home, and related to this is the desire for children. Sentiments, then, are groups of organized tendencies toward objects, ideas, and people. Desires, sentiments and attitudes are the "drives" of a person's life.

Judging from their testimonies, these desires, sentiments, and attitudes were changed. The criminal's whole attitude was changed toward Christ; the desire of the medical doctor for alcohol was taken away; the prostitute wanted her baby; and the minister's sentiments toward the gospel, which were grouped around ethics and social justice, was changed to the gospel which is "the living Christ." In general their sentiments, desires, and attitudes, which had been centered in worldly objects, interests, people, and ideas, were now centered on Jesus and His gospel. In other words, in every true conversion, the power of the old "drives" of life are broken, and a new set of values, of interests, of attitudes and of sentiments are created. Therefore, if any man be in Christ, he is a new creation; the old has passed away, behold the new has come (II Cor. 5:17).

You tell me, therefore, that you are a Christian. Then examine yourself, as Paul commands, "to see if you are in the faith." Did you experience an impression or emotion of joy, love, comfort and peace? Did there come a consciousness of a lifted burden, and a freedom from a sense of guilt at the moment of conversion? Also, has there been any change in your attitudes, sentiments, and desires? For example, do you hold hostility or an unforgiving spirit toward anyone? Do you now desire to give to help the cause of Christ, to read the Bible, to pray, and to attend church services? In short, and in general, would you now rather live to please the Lord Jesus than to please yourself? If you can give a positive answer to these questions, then you have the experience Mark of a Christian.

A word of caution should be given at this point. No two people are born with the same degree of mental powers. We differ with reference to our attitudes, sentiments, temperaments, strength of will, and sensitiveness of conscience. As a result of these differences, no two conversions will be the same. However, the fundamental principles by which one may enter the kingdom of God, such as decision, repentance, and faith, will be the same for everyone. The application of these conditions will differ with different people. Also the evidence of conversion from experience, such as the consciousness of Christ's presence in the soul, and the impressions of love and peace, will differ in intensity with different people. A person can, then, be truly born of the Spirit with but little or no outward demonstration and no deep emotions of love and joy. Bear in mind, however, that the Holy Spirit, in His own way, will testify to these quiet conversions that they have experienced the new birth.

CHAPTER THREE

The Marks of a Christian from Scripture

"It is true that in the soul of the regenerated there is a vital principle, but the source of its energy is outside of ourselves in Christ. There is indwelling but not interpretation. (His life does not penetrate or spread through the human spirit but forms a union with it.) The dweller and his house are distinct. Hence in the regenerated man life is extraneous (outside of himself), its seat is not in himself—. To obtain gas from the city gas works is one thing; to manufacture it at one's own cost in one's own establishment is quite another. The regenerated child of God receives life direct from Christ, who is outside of him at the right hand of God, through the channels of faith." (Abraham Kuyper)

"One thing I know, that whereas I was blind, now I see" (John 9:25).

Scriptural Evidence of the New Birth

In a previous chapter, a Christian was defined as one to whom has been imparted Spiritual Life or the life of Christ. This event can be known in two ways; by experience, which has been discussed, and direct statements from the Bible. Let us now turn to the Scriptures for more evidence of the Marks of a Christian.

This question now comes to mind: How do you stand at the present moment in your relation to Christ—weeks, months, years—after that initial contact? The following passages of Scripture will help answer that question.

First, the love mark, I John 3:14. "We have passed from death unto life because we love the brethren." The word "love" in the Greek is *agapas*. It is a type of love that comes from Christ. The love a mother feels toward her child, or a husband and wife toward each other, is a different kind than Christian love. Such a love swells up from within. It is aroused or brought to life when one person meets or comes in contact with another person. However,

Christian love springs up within only when communion or correspondence is established with Christ. Human love, in a sense, is selfish and in time will cease to exist. Christian love has in it the elements of eternity. It is an all inclusive love, and it embraces not only Christians but even one's enemies. It is a marvelous fact, then, to know that the love of Christ or the life of Christ in me is the same person that is in every Christian. Because of this fact, there is a different kind of affinity and unity between Christians than exists between non-Christians.

In order, then, for the Christian to measure himself by this love mark, two things should be considered. The first is what could be called a negative aspect. Do you, as a Christian, possess or practice such traits as unjustifiable anger, hostility, resentment, impatience, jealousy and all such traits? This does not necessarily mean that spiritual life has not been imparted to you. It does mean that all such traits are incompatible with the Christian life. They must go, by the help of the Spirit, or they will hinder the growth of those opposite traits given in the 13th Chapter of I Corinthians. Paul warns every Christian that those who are motivated by hostility, strife, worldly pleasures, adultery and so on, shall not inherit the Kingdom of God.

On the positive side of the love mark which will help one to determine his standing with Jesus is I Corinthians chapter 13. In this chapter, Paul gives nine ingredients of love. Among them are patience, politeness, good-temper, kindness, humbleness, is not jealous, delights not in evil, and harboring no evil thoughts.

Measure, then, your standing with Christ with this measuring ruler of love. If by the help of the Spirit, you are seeking to eliminate every evil trait and cultivate in your daily life the ingredients of Christian love you possess the love mark of a Christian.

As another Mark of a Christian consider I John 3:24. "Whosoever practices obedience to his commands remains in union with Him and he in union with him; and in this way we *know* that he remains in union with us, by the Spirit that He has given to us."

One of the most comforting evidences that one is a Christian is a consciousness of Christ's presence in the soul. As has been said, a Christian is one who possesses a life which before his contact with Christ, he did not possess. This *Life* is Christ Himself. That one, then, who possesses this life or who has formed a union with Christ will be conscious or will know that Christ dwells within. And the depth or intensity of this conscious knowledge will differ with different people and at different times with the same Christian. If one, therefore, is a Christian, he will be able to detect the Spirit's presence. The same truth is taught in I John 4:13. "Hereby know we that we dwell in Him, and He in us, because He has given us of his Spirit." Remember, the Holy Spirit is a personality. As a person, He makes His presence known through our conscience by approving or condemning our conduct; through our sensibilities by bringing comfort, and peace; and through our intellect which enables us to think, reason and thus to *know* our standing with Him. If, therefore, from time to time, you can detect within strange impressions or movements of comfort even in the midst of trouble, you will know, as John tells us, that the Holy Spirit is at work in the soul. This means also that you are a child of God.

So far we have considered this issue of the Marks of a Christian from the standpoint of God. The work of the Spirit enables the Christian to know his relationship with Christ. But what part, if any, does the Christian play in maintaining this relationship? To answer this question, let us go back to I John 3:24. "Whosoever practices obedience to his commands—." In John 8:51 are these words: "Verily, verily, I say unto you, if a man keep (*Tereo*, retain and observe) my word, he shall never see death." Also in I John 2:3 are found these words: "Hereby we know that we know Him, if we keep his commandments."

The purpose of keeping the commandments is to regulate conduct, and their number and variety are such as to govern every aspect of life. They can be classified under such headings as social, economic, government, and Christianity. For example, "Let him that stole, steal no more" (Eph. 4:28), pertains in general to economic and sets the limit on how to obtain property and all of life's necessities; the golden rule governs our conduct in our social relationships; and obey those who have rule over you— (Heb.

13:17). Every citizen is to render obedience to his government when such obedience is not in conflict with a clear command of God. And "thou shall worship the Lord thy God and Him only shall thou serve," has to do with our object of worship. Everyone has some supreme object of love. Corresponding to an inner desire to love and worship something is some object outside of us. This could be wife, husband, children, position of power, or money in all its forms, and finally the Lord Jesus Christ. As the years advance from childhood to, say middle age, some one of the above objects will crystalize into a supreme love. What folly then, to center our affection on some object which in time will fade away. For the Christian, therefore, Christ and Him only, must head the list of those things from which he draws his earthly pleasure and happiness. All this does not mean that we should love husband, wife, children, and so on, less but rather, when a choice must be made between these objects of affection and Jesus, the decision must be in His favor.

The commandments of God can also be classified as negative and positive commands. All are familiar with such negative commands (those we should not do) as the ten commandments. These ten commandments are so broad in their application as to cover the most important negative aspects of human and divine relationships. The two most prevalent violations of these commands, among all classes of people, including Christians, are lying and stealing. These can be done in a dozen different ways. For example, not reporting an item on your income tax report is another form of stealing; keeping silent when the occasion demands that we should speak could be a form of lying; and refusing to acknowledge Christ as our Saviour, by word or action, when the situation demands it, is not only denying Him but is also another form of lying.

There is another form of lying and stealing about which the Christian must be on his guard. This has to do with a company, corporation, government, or some organized body. For some, even Christians, regard it as permissible to cheat and steal when from an individual they would not do so. The keeping, therefore, of these negative commands are not burdensome for that Christian, who determines by the help of the Spirit, to make decisions which Christ will approve.

On the positive side, the commandments are not less binding. Before considering them, here once more, is a list of some of the positive commandments: I John 3:24, John 8:51, I John 2:3, and Luke 8:15. All these verses indicate that faithful obedience of the commandments or the keeping of His word, once heard and received, is the way of continued deliverance and salvation.

Let us turn now to one of the great positive commands of Christ. It is found in John 15:4. In fact, John 15:1-6 contains the foundation principle which governs the relation of Christ to the individual. "For the believer is a living participation proceeding upon a living faith, in a living Saviour. The principle is reduced to its simplest statement in the words of Jesus, abide in me, and I in you." This abiding in Christ is a fundamental requirement of every Christian. In fact, to possess His life is impossible without abiding in Him. To determine your relation to Christ, let us see just what abiding in Him really means.

The Greek word for abide is *Meno*—dwell, remain, continue. Each of these words can be substituted for abide. To abide or to dwell in Christ and He in us means:

(1) Our life comes from Him. The whole of salvation is not wrapped up in the initial experience of the new birth. Jesus speaking in John 6:56, said, (Williams translation) "Whosoever continues to eat my flesh and drink my blood continues to *live in union* with me and I in union with him. Just as the living Father has sent me and I live because of the Father, so whoever keeps on eating me will live because of me." Just as the body cannot continue to live without food being taken into it from without, so the Christian cannot continue to live in union with Christ without partaking of the life which issues from Him. Exactly what is this spiritual food which Jesus symbolically says is His flesh? It is actually a Spiritual force, a power, which the Christian can appropriate by a study of the Bible, by prayer, by making decisions which Jesus will approve, by good works, and by practicing the ingredients of love as given in the 13th chapter of I Corinthians. This Spiritual power, to repeat, though unseen is as real as the magnetic waves which

activate the motor that lifts the garage door. However, unlike such waves, which are dead and lifeless, this power proceeds from a person—the Holy Spirit. By His help, that Christian, who is determined to follow Christ, will be able to make use or appropriate that Spiritual power upon which abiding in Christ depends. If, therefore, his life or nourishment is flowing from Christ, the vine to you, the branch, through the channels of faith, you are abiding in Christ.

There is another point the Christian should remember in regard to Christ dwelling in the Christian. Abiding in Christ is a command. And the Christian's obedience to this command depends upon his own volition. That one, then, who habitually engages in sinful conduct, who turns his back on Christ for some worldly pleasure or who simply neglects to partake of the food which will nourish his soul, can no longer be said to abide in Christ.

The extent of keeping the commandments, is, therefore, evidence of one's union with Christ. And we have not meant to imply that they must be obeyed perfectly. In a world of outward evil, and a tendency within toward sinful conduct, this is impossible. However, there is an area within from which all forms of evil originate. That area has to do with purposes, motives, and intentions. A motive is an inner drive or impulse that causes one to act in a certain way. Purpose and intent have meanings similar to motive. It is these three factors of the mind that determines whether conduct is sinful. To take human life, for example, is not murder if done unintentionally; and to tell an untruth is not lying unless the motive is to deceive. To repeat, due to faulty judgment, mistakes, and so on, the Christian's conduct in all areas of living will not be perfect. However, in this realm of the heart where the "drives" of life have their origin, the Christian can live above sin. For the living Spirit abides in this area and sin cannot enter except by the permissive will of the Christian.

The Assurance of Faith

In I John 5:10, this verse is found: "He that believes on the Son of God has the witness (or the assurance) in himself." This verse is in harmony with Romans 8:16.

Notice, the word *believe* has two aspects. The first is to accept as true that a man like Jesus lived, performed miracles, was crucified, and rose from the dead. This can be called faith of the intellect. But it is not that faith or belief that results in the imparting of spiritual life to the soul. The other aspect of believing on the Son is a mental act of submission to Christ. To submit to Christ involves three things: (1) A decision to follow Him, (2) Repentance—a determination to give up any conduct He will not approve, (3) Confession—seeking forgiveness for sinful conduct. All this is known as faith of the heart. Faith of the intellect and faith of the heart together is believing on the Son.

As a Christian, then, you have sought the Lord and found Him by believing on the Son. However, that initial experience of forgiveness was only the beginning of your Christian life. Believing on the Son is not merely the work of a moment. The verbs *hath* and *believe* are in the present tense and in Greek denotes continued action. I John 5:10, then should read: "He that believes (He that believes now and continues to believe) hath (and continues to have) the witness in himself." Have you tried to right that wrong you did to another and also asked for divine forgiveness? In spite of suffering and loss, do you still retain your faith in God? If so the Spirit, in His own way, will give you the assurance of the faith Mark of a Christian.

Other Evidence of Sonship

Four other verses will be mentioned by which one can test his relationship with Christ. This relationship, then, can be tested by the change which has taken place. "I know that whereas I was blind now I see." No greater evidence is possible of an inward change than experience. The outward ability of this man to see or change is evidence beyond dispute of an inward change. Spiritual life is imparted within an area of the soul. This Life is not static or passive. It immediately begins its work of regeneration. This inward Life of Christ is silent and unseen. No outside person can know the moment of His arrival or of His continued existence in the soul. The dwelling of Christ in the heart can, then, be known to the Christian and an outsider by a change in attitudes and conduct.

I John 3:19 is another verse by which the Christian can test his standing with Jesus. "And we *know* that we are of God, and the whole world lieth in wickedness." Contrast your state of heart with your non-Christian friends and relatives. They may be good moral people who are honest and trustworthy in their business and social relationships. Yet there will be a subtile difference in outlook, a leaning toward worldly things and a shying away from a holy and righteous life on the part of a non-Christian. This is only natural because of the enmity of the carnal mind toward Christ. The Christian, however, can *know* that he is justified by faith because he feels no enmity—no hostility toward Christ or the living of a righteous life.

Again, the Christian can know his present relationship with Christ by his fruits. It can be said there are two types or varieties of fruit mentioned in the New Testament. One is fruit of the Spirit. In Galatians 5:22, 23, nine different kinds are mentioned, such as peace, longsuffering, faith, joy, meekness, and temperance. The other type has to do with words and actions. As given in Philippians 1:11. "As Jesus Christ has filled your life with righteous works by which you glorify and praise God" (Beck's Translation). Not only then, are the fruits of the Spirit inward traits as those given above, but also outward fruit or works such as giving to Christian schools, churches, helping others, visiting those in prisons, praying for those who know not the Lord Jesus, and so on. This list can also be said to be fruits of the Spirit, for they are simply outward expressions of inward traits of faith, patience, temperance and so on. If, therefore, when the Christians, by contrast with his friends and relatives who are non-Christians, discovers he is bearing, though imperfectly, the fruit of a Christian, then let him be assured he has the fruit mark of a Christian.

The Denial of Self

Aside from the marks of a Christian given above, the strength of the ties which binds one to Christ can be tested in another way. This method is known as self-denial or the denying of self. The authority for this neglected method is a verse found in Matthew 16:24. "If any man would come after me, let him deny himself, take up his cross and follow me."

According to Webster, the "self" means our identity, character, or personality. It is I myself. Him is a pronoun which refers to man. Him, then, the man, is superior to and capable of saying *no* to that part of "himself"—that inward region of emotions, attitudes, and desires which are antagonistic to or in conflict with Him. The Christian or non-Christian who would follow Jesus must say now to that "self" who would rebel against Christ.

As a Christian, the first great victory over sin occured when first one submitted his life to Christ. However, this did not end the conflict with *self*. In some respects, it was only the beginning. For as a new convert, the power of evil to control the Christian has been broken. Yet old habits, desires, and tendencies toward sin still linger.

The question arises as to how best these remnants of the old life can be dealt with. They must be stamped out and destroyed or they will seek to encroach on the territory of the New Life and cause trouble if not estrangement from Christ. Warnings against this possibility have been given time and again especially by Jesus and Paul. "If we," says Paul, "live after the flesh, we shall die." And Jesus commands the Christian to dwell or abide in Him. And if we deny Him, He will deny us. The only safe and secure path to follow is, then, to deny ourselves those things that Jesus will not approve, however pleasurable and satisfying they may be.

How to Deny "Himself" or Self

There are three methods the Christian can use to deny himself. Authority for the use of these methods will be given. Both Paul and Jesus speak, in the passages quoted, as though the Christian's salvation depends entirely upon him. This, however, is not true. The Living Spirit is ever near. And so long as you, the Christian, do not make a deliberate decision to follow Christ no more, or to depart from Him by persistently and wilfully practicing sinful conduct, the Spirit will be faithful to you.

(1) In dealing, therefore, with the old nature, the first step, as strange and drastic as it may seem, is to die to a part of himself. If the Christian is to live unto God, he must die unto sin (Romans 7:9-11), or he must die to that part

of himself which would lead to sinful conduct. The Christian, then, must kill sin or it will kill him. Jesus, in Matthew 18:8-9, expressed the idea in these words: "Wherefore if thy hand or thy foot offend you (cause you to sin) cut them off—. And if thine eye offend you pluck it out—." Jesus in these vivid, symbolic words tells the Christian how to deal with certain emotions, attitudes, and desires. They must be dealt with in the most drastic way possible: a quick and sudden death. This is the best and perhaps the only way that some sinful activities or some of life's pleasures can be renounced.

It is difficult to give examples of those things which should meet a sudden death. For what is troublesome and should be cut off is not the same for each Christian. And what the Lord would approve in one Christian, He may not approve in another. An example of this, is that one, whom the Spirit beyond a doubt, has called to be a missionary or to enter some other kind of Christian work. This could mean cutting himself off from an ambitious promising career, the renouncing of a profitable business or a well-paying position in public or private life.

Consider now a general example of a Christian woman who is strongly attracted to a non-Christian man of doubtful reputation. The leading of the Spirit is such as to convince her not to marry him. She is aware that her love for him would cause her to sin. As painful as it may be, to obey the Spirit, she must deal with her affection by severing at once relations with him.

Another example of this command has to do with habits which may or may not have been formed before the new birth. These are common habits such as use of tobacco, drugs, overeating, observing questionable forms of entertainment, and sexual liberties which could lead to sinful conduct. All such habits are, therefore, incompatible with the life of a Christian. And Jesus, in the above verses, states that, like an infected eye or hand, to save the whole body, they must be cut off at once.

These are therefore, habits, desires, and attitudes (attitudes are learned tendencies to behave in a certain way toward objects, persons and ideas) which if retained, Jesus would not approve. The only sensible and humane method to deal with them is to kill them. This is done by severing all contacts and relations with them. As time, then, moves onward, the Christian discovers that he must relinquish some love, some cherished desire which may not be wrong in itself but which, in a subtle way, hinders the Spirit in the development of Christian character. The giving up, therefore, for Christ's sake, those activities, persons or things, that we may love as our eye, is the practicing of self-denial.

(2) Another way of denying *self* is known as mortification. The authority for this method is Paul's statement in Roman's 8:5-13. The Greek word to *mortify* is *nekroo*. As a verb, it means to put to death, kill, to deaden. One of its meanings in English is to become gangrenous. the word, then, carries with it the idea of a slow rather than a quick, sudden way of dying. Mortification is, then, a gradual loosing of the tentacles of evil desires and tendencies of the disposition. This meaning of the word corresponds with its use when applied to a diseased member of our body. If, for example, one's hand is infected, it could be the only way to save the remaining of the body is to cut off the hand. However, this would be of no good if the infection has spread to other parts of the body. But if a member of our spiritual body is infected with the virus, for example, of covetousness, it can only be eliminated by the process of mortification. The knife is of no value here.

In Colossians 3:5, Paul gives five traits of the law or principles of sin. These are: Immorality—sexual deviations of all kinds: impurity—good deeds intermingled with sinful conduct: covetousness—a worship of money; passion—strong desire such as sexual lusts: and evil desire—hostility, jealousy, envy, revenge and so on.

With reference to these lingering elements of sin in a Christian, it is clear that he will not be troubled by all of them. Each will discover that he has a fault, a weakness, some compelling desire which he discovers as his "besetting sin." This may or may not be the same as another.

Aside from the list above, one of the common characteristics of the old "self" is sensitiveness. That Christian with an over-sensitive disposition will see insults when none is intended; simple misunderstandings will often lead to hostility and estrangement even between Christians;

and since the action and words of others cannot be controlled, such a person is constantly at odds with others. Now notice, one way for the Christian to "grow in grace" is to give heed to constructive criticism. For often the Christian is blind to his faults and sins. This criticism, when heeded, leads to the development of Christian character. That Christian, then whose "feelings are easily hurt," will tend to become angry and will defend himself and turn way from advice given even by the Apostle Paul.

Another fault which can lead to sinful conduct in words and deeds is an angry, irritable, and fault-finding disposition. Such people have a real fight on their hands to maintain that calmness of spirit which should characterize every Christian. This state of the heart is, also, associated with an oversensitive spirit. Then too, it is often with wife, husband, and children that this sensitiveness and irritability is most noticeable. As a Christian, you are aware that this condition of the heart must be eliminated. And this elimination is not a sudden cutting off of a tendency or trait which can lead to sinful conduct, but a slow dying out to these things known as mortification. Otherwise they will tend to alienate you from Christ.

(3) The third method of dealing with the roots of sin is limitation. This method has to do with those emotions, attitudes and desire which are not sinful in themselves up to a point. But the satisfying of certain desires beyond that point, the Lord will not approve. That one, then, who has made Christ the Lord and Master of his life will discover certain activities can be sinful if engaged in beyond certain limits.

Consider some examples of limitation in dealing with sinful conduct. "The love of money," said Paul, I Timothy 6:10, "is the root of all evil." There is, then, no sin or no disapproval of the love of money up to a point. Just where that point lies must be determined by each Christian. In general the Christian who refuses to purchase what he and his family need because of his desire to "lay up money" or goes to the other extreme and contracts debts when such debts could be avoided; who, where money is involved, operates on the border-line of dishonesty; and who refuses to give, what can be given, to Christian charity—then he has gone beyond the point where his love for money is greater than his love for Christ.

A second example of limitation has to do with the natural love which the Christian holds for others. This will include the affection which he holds for husband, wife, children, friends and relatives. However, for the Christian, there is another who lays claim to his supreme love—Jesus Christ. Jesus in Luke 14:26, says plainly; "If any come to me, and hate not his father, and mother, and wife, and children, and brethren, and sister, yea, and his own life also, he cannot be my disciple." The Greek word for "hate" is *miseo*. It means to love less. Jesus is, then, saying here that the Christian is not to love his family, relatives, and friends less, but to love Him more. The test of discipleship, therefore, would come when, as His follower, the Christian must choose between some loved one and Christ. The Christian's love must, then, be limited to Christ alone.

By way of summary, there is in all men a principle of evil or law of sin which is opposed to Christ. When Christ makes His appearance in the soul at conversion, the power of this law of sin to control conduct is broken. The roots or scattered remnants of this law of sin are still present to hinder the growth of Christian character.

Bear in mind, it is not isolated acts of evil, such as lying, with which we are now concerned. Rather, it is the law of sin or the principle of evil. Let the Christian, by the help of the Spirit, control or eliminate this law of sin from the heart and isolated acts of evil will take care of themselves.

The whole idea is to "kill sin" or it will kill you. To accomplish this process of dying, some evil traits can best be dealt with by a sudden stoppage. "If thy eye cause you to sin pluck it out—." As an example of this method, there are certain habits that slowly tend to wreck body and mind. The best way to deal with them is to cut them off as swiftly as you cut off your hand or pluck out your eye. Other desires of this inward rebellious principle, can be destroyed only by slow degree as an infected sore. This is known as mortification. And an example is a temper difficult to control.

Now this question: Just how does the Christian go about applying these methods of "killing" these remnants of the old nature? First, the Christian must be made aware that they exist, and that their existence in the soul is a continual hindrance to living a life pleasing to Christ. How, the Holy Spirit does not tell us, as a usual thing, in an audible voice, or send an angel to tell the Christian of his sinful traits and desires. All that is necessary for him to become aware of them is to notice how he *reacts* to conditions and circumstances which occur in his surroundings. One person, for example, will react to his need for money by stealing it; a husband will react to his desire for another woman by divorcing his wife. Or some outward object, condition, or person can arouse an inward evil desire such as greed, jealousy, revenge, lust, and so on. However, such desires may not be satisfied or acted upon. Yet that does not, from the standpoint of God, make them any less sinful. As a Christian, then, as you live your life from day to day, you will be made aware, especially by what people say and do to you, of some elements of the old nature.

Second, now that you know you possess some such trait (if you really do) as those mentioned above, read what the Scripture says concerning them. Two verses will be given; one in I John 1:9, the other in I John 1:7. In both verses, the promise is made that you can be freed from those roots of sin such as hostility. But in both verses the freeing or cleansing from wrong conduct is based on certain conditions. The condition in I John 1:9 is confessing of sins; in I John 1:7 it is "walking in the light." The result which follows a confession is divine forgiveness and cleansing. This cleansing, promised in both verses, includes the elimination of all evil traits or desires.

Third, the above verses and others clearly teach that the Christian need not go through life troubled by some element of sin. However, the Spirit will not do His work unless you, as a Christian, call upon Him for help, determine not to yield to desires that can lead to sinful conduct, and seek for forgiveness when a wrong is done.

Conclusion

Here, then, in the realm of self-denial is the criterion by which the Christian can judge the degree of his spiritual condition. Everyone, to some extent, must practice self-denial. This is done either to please ourselves or to please Christ. To receive credit for any form of self-denial, the motive of the Christian must be to please Christ. If, then, you cut yourself off from those things you love as your eye, habitually refuse to satisfy desires which Christ will not approve and allow them to die a natural death, and remember to limit the satisfying of those desires and activities which Christ does approve, then this denying of *self* is evidence of a saving relationship with Christ.

A Changed Life

There is another mark of a Christian which is usually open and visible for everyone to see. and this mark has to do with a changed life. And this evidence concerns both experience and Scripture. Also the changed life concerns not only the beginning of the New Birth but from that moment to the end of life.

There are two ways a person can change. One way is known as regeneration; the other is known as reformation. Let us first define regeneration.

Regeneration is a change in the character for a person by the agency of the Holy Spirit. My part in the act of regeneration is to yield to the conviction of the Spirit by being willing to confess my sins, determine not to repeat them, and trust the Lord to impart His life to me. Also in regeneration, which means the same as being born again, the tendency to engage in evil conduct is removed, or the dominion which sin has over one in his natural state is broken and abolished. It is that renewal of our nature which gives us dominion over the tendency to sin and enables us to serve God from love and not from fear.

Notice that regeneration is an inward change of attitudes and desires. And this change will result in the bestowal of an inward power to resist and destroy evil impulses and desires. For a person to regenerate himself, it should be remembered, is impossible. It is the work of the Spirit but always with our consent.

Now, it is possible for a person by sheer will power to change his conduct. This is known as reformation. There can be reformation without regeneration, but there can be no regeneration without reformation. Reformation is an outer work; regeneration is an inner. There is a difference in whitewashing and washing white. Reformation has to do with conduct; "in regeneration the old vessel is not repaired and repainted; rather it is remelted and remolded." A change to be of value must begin within and work without. That person, then, who, for example, has ceased to lie, to smoke, to drink, to give up adulterous conduct and so on, because such conduct affects his business, his health, his reputation, or his home life, then it can be said he has reformed. However, if these same things are not indulged in, not because of outward considerations, but because of an inward change brought about by the Holy Spirit, then this is regeneration.

The same thing can be said on the positive side. If you attend church, give to help the poor, don't cheat in your business and so on, but do these things to please yourself, then you stand on the side of reformation. However, if these same things are done simply because of your love for and the desire to please Christ, then you have experienced regeneration.

As a professed Christian, examine your relationship with Christ in the light of reformation and regeneration. The idea to bear in mind is not that each will achieve the same beneficial results, but what is the motivation behind the changes in conduct. If those changes in your life are the result of an indwelling Christ, then rest assured that such changes are the mark of a Christian.

CHAPTER FOUR

Deception Pertaining to the New Birth

"She was in a most dangerous position; she believed herself to be awake and healthy, but she was cold and frozen. What little life she had was fast ebbing away, and she was sleeping quietly the sleep of death."

"Examine yourselves to see if you really believe. Test yourselves. Don't you know Jesus Christ is in you—unless you fail the test?" (II Cor. 13:5).

Deception and Decision

As was said in a previous chapter, a Christian is one to whom has been imparted the life of Christ by the agency of the Holy Spirit. Or John speaks of the experience as one to whom Christ has come to dwell. Regardless, then, of the profession a person may make, if Christ, His spirit or His life is not present in the soul, he cannot be a Christian. It has also been shown that both, from the standpoint of Scripture and experience, one can know that moment or hour when Christ comes to the soul. Yet as contradictory as it may seem, it is possible for one to be deceived relative to his union with Christ.

That one, then, is deceived with respect to his relationship with Christ who insists that spiritual life has been imparted to him when in fact this experience has never occurred. This could be due to the Christian environment in which he grew up; it could be due to a false concept of who is a Christian; to erroneous beliefs learned from false teachers; or to the tenacity with which false ideals of religion grip the human mind. This last cause is the reason why, for example, millions of followers of Mohammed will never become Christians.

To repeat, the first requirement for one who would become a Christian is to decide to follow Christ. And to follow Christ or to "walk in the Spirit" means to make those decisions in all the affairs of life, that Christ will approve. However, the moment a person makes the decision to follow Christ does not necessarily mean he is now a Christian. One of the deceptions of being born again lies at this point. For the moment of decision and the moment of the new birth could be, and often are, at different times. It is possible, then, for one seeking Christ to be deceived into believing he has experienced the new birth on the basis of his decision alone. This could be true depending on the person. To determine your spiritual condition consider the evidence as given in a previous chapter. This is Scriptural and experimental evidence. The evidence from Scripture can be summed up in the word *believe*. To believe on Christ means to trust His word, to tell Him or to be willing to tell Him, that you have lied, stolen and so on, and to give up any conduct He will not approve. From experience you can know that you have "passed from death into life" by the impressions of joy, peace, comfort and love which follow the advent of spiritual life in the soul. These emotions or impressions will vary in intensity with different people. From this evidence, you can rest assured of being a child of God. If, however, you simply make a decision and state you now accept Christ as your Saviour, yet there is no confession of sins, only as half-hearted giving up of activities which Christ will not approve, no testimony of His saving grace, no conscious knowledge of His presence in your soul at any time, and the whole bent of your life is to live to please yourself—then to all appearance you are deceived in believing you are a Christian on the basis of your decision alone.

The Moral Man and the Christian

Another area of deception has to do with the moral man and the Christian. To understand the nature of this deception, it is necessary to compare the two. This comparison will be made under four headings. They are:

(1) The moral man can be a person of great moral beauty. He will manifest in his daily conduct such qualities as kindness, love, compassion, generosity and so on. Perhaps, these traits will be manifest to a greater degree than in some Christians. In fact if only the above traits were considered, it would be difficult, like the tares and wheat, to distinguish the two.

(2) The person of high moral character approves and delights in truth and justice. He is ready, at any time, to defend that one who has been or is being treated unfairly. His sense of fairness and justice extends to government, business, social relationships, and in all human affairs. The Christian also insists that justice and truth prevail regardless of race, social and business prestige and family relationships.

(3) Attitudes are very important in determining conduct. They are learned inclinations to behave in a certain way toward objects, persons, and ideas. Notice, you were not born with an attitude. It is a state or condition of mind that you learned from your parents, friends, teachers and so on. For example, in some way, you learned to lean toward or against the Republican party, the Negro, the Jews, abortion, and so on. It is clear that as far as moral issues are concerned, attitudes can be right or wrong. However, the good moral person will, with all such issues, lean in the direction of truth and honesty. Of course the Christian will do the same. To continue the example, a Christian's attitude toward money will simply be to regard it as a necessary tool in daily living. To him it will not become an idol, a supreme love, or as a means of acquiring power over people. Yet the man of noble moral qualities will in general assume the same attitude. With respect, also, toward good works, the Christian and the good moral man will possess the same attitude. They both will give to organizations such as the church, Christian schools, and the Red Cross. Both, also, will give not only money, but will help in other ways those whom charity organizations do not reach. These, then, are a few of many ways that good moral people and Christians are similar in their attitudes and activities.

However, that one of high moral character and the Christian do differ in some important respects. One of these differences has to do with motives. The motive of the Christian in all he does or doesn't do, and his attitudes, is to please Christ. When decisions must be made in regard to his business, social life, marriage, and everyday affairs, they are made with one thought in mind, to meet Christ's approval. However, the motive of the moral man in denouncing such things as abortion, dishonesty, sexual lusts, and giving to help those in need, is not to please Christ but himself. The good moral person condemns wicked conduct in all its forms from feelings of fear, disgust, and loathing. Also, the moral person is just and honest simply because it is the way he is constituted. The fact that Christ demands that he be just, honest, and regards sin as something to be rejected, has but little if anything to do with his conduct, state of mind, or attitudes. As stated before, at this point the good moral man could be deceived in believing that he is a Christian. Bear in mind, a Christian's purposes and motives in helping others, for example, are to yield obedience to the Lord. The good moral man, who may be a church member, may do the same thing without giving Christ a thought. He is yielding obedience not to Christ but to a law of his own nature.

(4) We have yet to state a fact of supreme importance concerning the moral man and the Christian. In spite of their similarities and differences in motives, there exists a fundamental difference between the person of the highest moral virtue and the Christian. What is this difference? To answer the question, the Christian has all those noble characteristics, in varying degrees, possessed by the moral man plus something else or some one else. And that something else is the divine life of Christ. The Christian, then, shares with Christ a life of peace and eternal happiness. The moral person can never partake of such a life since he does not possess it. One, then, is living; the other is dead. Spiritual death is a lack of contact or communion with God. The contacts of the moral person, in spite of his magnificent moral attributes, are limited to this physical world into which he was born. The growth, therefore, of his moral nature is limited to this present world. But who can set the limit on that divine life in the soul of the Christian? "It does not appear what it shall be—"

We are now in a better position to understand how morality can be confused with Christianity. It is possible, then, for that person who lives all but a blameless life to come to regard himself as a Christian when he has never entered the kingdom of God. Consider that person who has attended church services from childhood. He is fully aware of the life and teachings of that marvelous Person called Jesus Christ. He is fair, honest and upright in all his human relationships. He supports and upholds the doctrines of his church. Is it any wonder then that this man of noble moral attributes, over the months or years, comes to regard himself as a Christian?

A close scrutiny, however, may reveal his true position. His attitudes in general will be determined by factors other than what Christ approves or disapproves. For example, the attitude of the good moral person, who also is known as a man of the world, is to regard money only as an instrument by which material possessions can be obtained. With regard to questionable issues such as the use of tobacco, worldly pleasure, and sharp business deals, he will lean in that direction without giving a thought as to whether Christ approves these activities. The moral man, also, who thinks of himself as a Christian may secretly if not openly deny that holiness of heart and righteousness in conduct are the goals of the Christian life. In general this moral person will lack the demeanor of that humble Christian whose life is controlled by the conscious presence of God. All this indicates that the moral person, regardless of his Christian-like activities, is in a state of Spiritual death. "—I know your deeds, that you have a name that you are alive, and you are dead." (Rev. 3:1).

Deception and Church Membership

Perhaps, in the whole realm of Christian deception none is more pronounced than in church membership. In order to get at the truth with reference to this type of deception, let us again repeat that a Christian is a person to whom has been imparted a *life* which before he did not possess. This life or Spiritual energy is as real as waves of television which move through the air with the speed of light. This *life* can be identified. We know what it is or who it is. It is Christ. He came to me and lives in some mysterious way within me. I knew, by the love, joy, and peace I experienced the moment He came to me. His coming did not, however, destroy my personality; I am still Earl Robinson with all the mental powers with which I was born. However, the most radical change occurred in the whole sweep of my personality when He shifted the desire to live to please myself from myself to Him. Among, then, of all the created beings of earth or heaven, Christ comes first in all the affairs of my life. In return for my love and loyalty to Him, He gives me a conscious knowledge of His presence, peace of mind even in the midst of trouble, and the help to meet all the needs of life. All these things, therefore, are the results of the "Life of Christ" in the soul and it is this Life within that makes the Christian.

Now notice, a church can be defined as a group of organized people who hold as true certain religious beliefs. Any church, then, that does not teach that conversion, the new birth, or regeneration occurs when *Christ, His Spirit*, or *His Life* comes to dwell in the soul is a *false* church. And I do not mean His coming is in some symbolic way. Rather, this type of Life is as real as the physical life we possess. And just as physical life makes the man, so the Life of Christ, to repeat, makes the Christian. In general, therefore, the members of that church which does not include in its tenets of faith the above definition of a Christian are deceived in believing they are Christians when in fact, they are strangers to the experience of the new birth.

But this is not all. Many churches or denominations do include in their tenets of faith the belief that only that one in whom Christ dwells is a Christian. However, the lives of many members of such churches do not measure up to the "Marks of a Christian." Yet somehow they are *deceived* in believing they are Christians just because they are members of an organized body of believers called a church, and also because they have lived and are living an all but blameless moral life.

This type of deception is especially dangerous to the spiritual welfare of such members. This could be due to three reasons. First, those in authority in the church such as pastors, priests, and teachers may never themselves have established a saving relationship with Christ. The results are simply the blind leading the blind. Second, since they may have been deceived for some time, it becomes difficult for even the Holy Spirit to awaken them to their true condition. Third, in due course of time, some of their deceived members may come to realize their true position.

They are not Christians. If they once possessed the life of Christ, they do so no longer and they know it. However, due to what they think will be adverse reaction by fellow members, friends, or relatives, they still pretend to be true followers of Christ.

Strange as it may appear, it is possible, therefore, for a person to be deceived with reference to his relationship with Christ. This deception pertains to a decision to submit to Christ; substituting moral goodness, including good works, for the regenerating life of Christ in the soul; and deception in regard to church membership.

A gifted writer has said, "No matter what may be the moral uprightness of his life, honorableness of his career, or the orthodoxy of his creed, if he exercises the function of living for the world, that defines his world—he cannot, in that case, belong to the higher kingdom."

No one need despair of knowing how he stands with reference to his relationship with Christ, or whether Christ abides within (see John 15:5). However, if you are one who has honest doubts as to this relationship, the difficulty could lay in one of two directions. First, you may never have experienced the saving grace of God. Go over again the evidence of Christ's presence with you as given in these pages. Such evidence will be along the line of experience and Scripture. Remember that saving faith is obedient faith. If you have made an irrevocable decision to follow Christ, you are willing to renounce every pleasure or give up anything else that he will not approve, confess *to Him* any sinful conduct and any inward sinful trait such as jealousy or hostility—if these conditions have been met, or you are willing to meet them, then you are believing on Jesus which means you will be saved. (Acts 16:31).

Second, you may be one who has in time past experienced the new birth. About this event in your life there is no doubt. However, that comfort of knowing that Christ will be near in time of trouble, and that peace of mind resulting from a consciousness of His presence, is gone. To seek out the difficulty between you and your Saviour, an examination is in order (II Cor. 13:5). Remember that sin, in some form, is the only thing that can separate you from Christ. If sin is found within the heart, or without in conduct it must be renounced, confessed, and a determination made not to repeat it. The Lord, then, will forgive and that comfort, peace, and friendship once known with the Saviour will return.

However, notice the other side; if on examination you discover no wilful practicing of sinful conduct, yet that feeling of estrangement from God still persists, then simply continue to seek and trust such promises as, "I will never leave you or forsake you." In due time the clouds of doubt and fears of a saving relationship with the Saviour will dissolve before the sunshine of His love, peace, and grace.